THE Leave It To Beaver™

GUIDE TO LIFE

THE Leave It To Beaver™

GUIDE TO LIFE

Wholesome Wisdom from the Cleavers!

RUNNING PRESS
PHILADELPHIA · LONDON

© 2006 Universal Studios Licensing LLLP
Leave It To Beaver is a copyright and trademark of Universal Studios. All Rights Reserved.
Printed in China

This book may not be reproduced in whole or in part, in any form or by any means, electronic or mechanical, including photocopying, recording, or by any information storage and retrieval system now known or hereafter invented, without written permission from the publisher.

9 8 7 6 5 4 3 2 1
Digit on the right indicates the number of this printing

Library of Congress Control Number: 2005937276

ISBN-13: 978-0-7624-2773-4
ISBN-10: 0-7624-2773-6

Written and edited by Jennifer Colella
Cover and interior designed by Corinda Cook
Typography: Caslon, Baskerville, Optima, Commercial Script, Brush Script, Gill Sans, Latin, Monotype Sorts, Carolina Brush, Havana, Pacific, Poppl Laudatio, Shelley, Snell Roundhand, Univers, and Typography of Coop

This book may be ordered by mail from the publisher. Please include $2.50 for postage and handling.
But try your bookstore first!

Running Press Book Publishers
125 South Twenty-Second Street
Philadelphia, Pennsylvania 19103-4399

Visit us on the web!
www.runningpress.com

Contents

Introduction

On October 4, 1957, the Soviet Union launched the world's first artificial

satellite, Sputnik, into outer space, ushering in a new era of political,

military, and technological developments. On that same day, television

audiences were captivated as they viewed life through the eyes of a

mischievous young boy named Beaver for the very first time. It was

a world on the verge of change, and *Leave It To Beaver*™ would become the

perfect bridge between the waning of old-time radio comedy and the blossoming of the television sitcom. Audiences watched. Audiences were entertained. And they learned something too!

On the surface, the Cleavers were a stereotypical family. Theodore "The Beaver" Cleaver symbolized the rambunctious innocence of childhood in a way that would make his character the stuff of TV legends. His

teenage brother, Wally, exemplified the slightly cranky yet mostly well-meaning older sibling. Ward Cleaver was a legitimate businessman and father who ventured out into the world to provide for his family, and June Cleaver remained the quintessential stay-at-home mom. While these roles are now seen as idyllic hallmarks of the era, it was how the family created and worked with these clichés that has made it a true classic for the ages. The experiences of the Cleavers reminded audiences that despite the challenges of life ahead, family, friendship, and good personal mottos would always be there to guide us.

As much as life has changed over the years, the show's simple and sweet observations have consistently reacquired appeal with new generations, and the wholesome wisdom of the Cleavers is now proven to be timeless.

Meet the Cleavers!

Ward Cleaver

As the head of the household (except when the kids are running amuck or when June puts her foot down), Ward Cleaver represents the nearly perfect family man. He's even-tempered, levelheaded, and always ready with advice for every situation. Remembering all too well his own boyhood days, Ward understands his sons and allows them to make mistakes and try out new things. He has experienced all

of the pitfalls of parenthood—alligators in the bathtub, unscrupulous kids, door-to-door sales, crazy parents, and every other imaginable worry and woe that accompanies growing children. Through it all, he's a loving father and a doting husband. While he is a successful businessman, family always comes first.

June Cleaver

The perfect 1950s mom, June Cleaver manages to rear two boys and a husband with grace and a lot of effort. She keeps an eye on the boys and home while Ward is at work—somebody has to watch the kids, or there might not be a home left to return to at the end of the day—and handles every situation kindly and sweetly. She takes on some of the most difficult parenting battles, including messy rooms, sibling squabbles, and good hygiene. Despite all of the time that goes into maintaining a family, June still manages to look her best and is always put together and fashionable. As a graduate from State College, she's also classy, intelligent, and the only thing that keeps Ward from being outnumbered by the boys.

Wallace "Wally" Cleaver

As the older and occasionally more mature brother, Wally encounters all of the difficulties of adolescence, including girls, friends, clubs, sports, and trying on occasion to disavow all knowledge of his family members. He's handsome, smart, athletic, and far more courteous than most boys his age. He's more worried about doing right than doing well, plus he's a fantastic brother most of the time. His best friend, Eddie Haskell, keeps him on his toes and in trouble, but Beaver is equally good at this. As the older brother, Wally is an important fountain of advice for Beaver, and sometimes for his parents as well.

Theodore "The Beaver" Cleaver

Being the youngest brother and baby of the family doesn't keep Beaver from trouble. He has a talent for all sorts of problems, such as losing money, notes, cats, and little girls, though he also proves to be clever and comes up with all sorts of ingenious ways to hide his mistakes. His plots into and out of trouble almost always entangle Wally, and he typically gets an earful of advice from the entire family. He tends to be goofy, hyperactive, and inquisitive, but he's mostly an average kid with a lot of friends. Some of his best adventures feature Beaver stuck in a tree, charging money to spit over a bridge, enamored with his teacher, painted a local hero, and falling into a soup bowl on a billboard.

Understanding Family

Time together can be as important as time apart.

June: C'mon, Beave, eat your peas.

Beaver: But I don't like the insides.

Wally: Well, then eat the outsides and shut up.

A family that eats together stays mad together.

June: Why don't you ever send me flowers?

Ward: I'm the kind that says it with seat covers.

Love is being able to say, "It's the thought that counts," while almost meaning it.

Beaver: Hey, Wally, why aren't mom and dad wearing these neat party hats?

Wally: 'Cause grownups have a lot harder time having fun at parties than kids do.

Party on, Cleaver-style!

Ward: You know, Beave, I used to walk to school when I was your age.

Beaver: Yeah, but every year the distance gets longer and the snow gets deeper.

PARENTS NEVER STRETCH THE TRUTH.

Clever Cleaver
Tricks for a
Wholesome Home
Tip #1

Innocent until proven
guilty just means that
you need to perfect the
art of looking innocent.

Beaver: But, it's my tree. I planted it. Can't I bring it to our new house?

June: Beaver, this tree belongs to someone else now. You can't take it with you.

If you love something, let it go.

ENCOURAGE
HOBBIES THAT
TEACH IMPORTANT
SKILLS LIKE
GETTING ALONG
WITH OTHERS,
TEAM WORK, AND
COOPERATION . . .

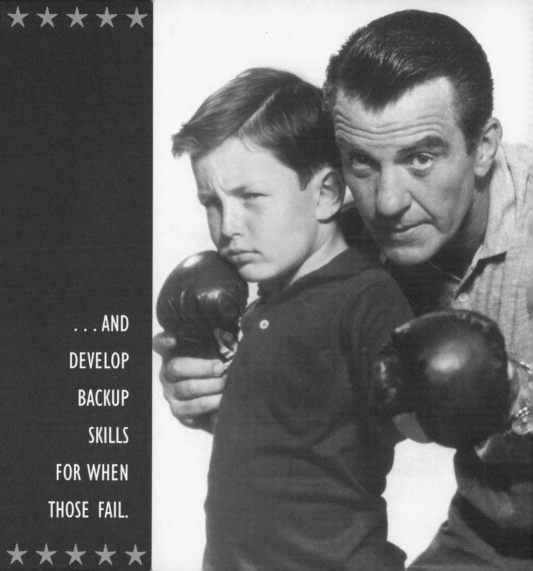

...AND DEVELOP BACKUP SKILLS FOR WHEN THOSE FAIL.

Beaver: You know what, Wally? I'm glad I don't know as much about life as you do. Otherwise, I'd be the biggest chicken in the whole world.

Wally: Well, golly Beave, why do you think I'm hiding out in the closet?

Ignorance is bliss.

Clever Cleaver
Tricks for a
Wholesome Home
Tip #2

Let your kids know that you're behind them every step of the way—literally behind them, watching their every move.

Don't turn your back on your family.

Steer a steady course.

June: I wish we could have gotten the message across with love and kindness.

Ward: Cheer up, June. If all else fails, we can always resort to that.

Always have a backup plan.

Ward: That's the trouble with kids. Just when you think you've built up a real understanding, a real man-to-man relationship, they turn around and start acting like . . . like . . .

June: Like children?

Acting your age can be fun!

Wally: If I had to have a brother, why'd it have to be an ape like you?

Beaver: You're a bigger ape!

Treat everybody with the love and kindness you'd show your brother or sister.

Surviving Friendship

If rational discussion doesn't work,
try hypnosis.

Eddie: So you are saying that it was wrong to chain Lumpy's transmission to a tree for fun?

Wally: Heck yeah. These types of jokes tend to backfire.

Eddie: No kidding.

Wally: Yeah, you creep.

With friends like these, who needs enemies?

June: You must be the new neighbors? Welcome to the neighborhood . . .

Don't worry about what you need to know in life. Instead, start to worry about whom you need to be friendly with.

Clever Cleaver
Tricks for a
Wholesome Home
Tip #3

When in doubt, present a united front and smile 'til it hurts.

Wally: Gee, Eddie, why are you always giving Beaver the business?

Eddie: I was just giving some advice to young Theodore.

Take advice with a smile and a grain of salt.

Wally: I don't get any of this.

Eddie: Who cares if you get it or not? Just copy the answers from my paper so we can get out of here.

Imitation is the sincerest form of friendship, and occasionally of cheating.

Clever Cleaver
Tricks for a
Wholesome Home
Tip #4

A good distance makes for good neighbors.

Wally: Boy, I'm really gonna clop him one.

A TRUE FRIEND
WILL
HAVE YOUR BACK,
EVEN AS
HE CLOPS YOU IN
THE FRONT.

Personal Mottos

If you want the job done right,
consider not doing it yourself.

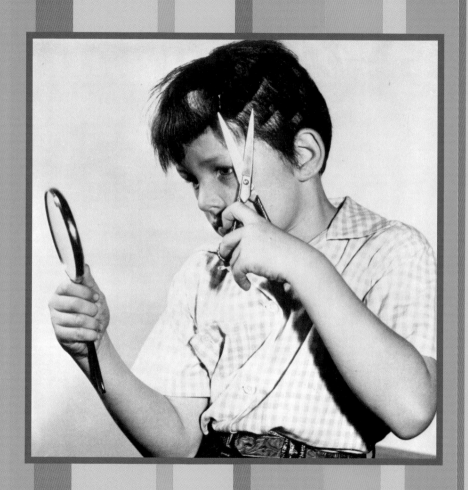

Ward: C'mon, Beave, be a soldier.

Beaver: If I were a soldier, I'd shoot the dentist.

You can't expect success without pulling some teeth.

Don't be afraid to go out on a limb.

Clever Cleaver
Tricks for a
Wholesome Home
Tip #5

Home is where the fresh food and free rent are.

It's never too late to come clean.

Beaver: I can't remember my lines with everybody looking at me.

Ward: Well now, Beaver, people look at you everyday and you certainly talk plenty in front of them.

All the world's a stage.

Wally: Wow, we got one.

Beaver: It's about time. I was beginning to think that the frogs were smarter than we were and that we'd never catch one.

Patience is a long-standing virtue because it requires long hours of standing.

Give a man a fish and he'll eat for a day; try to teach a man to fish and he may be hungry all afternoon.

Clever Cleaver
Tricks for a
Wholesome Home
Tip #6

The truth will set you free—right after you're properly punished for it.

Beaver: I wanted a horse and got a donkey instead.

Don't look a gift horse in the mouth.

Wally: Forget hot dogs. I should have stuck with Igloo bars.

Don't sweat the small stuff.

Beaver: The rules are a lot easier on grownups than they are on little boys.

Wally: Of course they are. Grownups are the ones that make the rules.

❖ ❖

Rules aren't always fair. The sooner you learn this, the sooner you can start breaking them.

Clever Cleaver
Tricks for a
Wholesome Home
Tip #7

June: Do you think all parents have this much trouble?

The grass is always greener in someone else's lawn.

If you are going to throw
someone a curveball,
try not to make it too obvious.

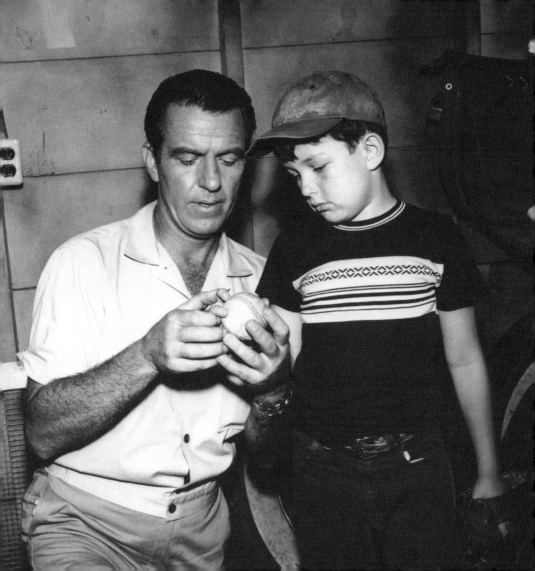

Beaver: Why do I have to have a lover-boy for a brother?

Wally: Why do you have to be such a slob?

Don't look down on those who look up to you.

And,
of course,
always
remember
the good
ole days
and the
wholesome
wisdom
of the
Cleavers!